IF I HAD A HAMMER
A Pete Seeger Singalong Songbook

Edited by
Annie Patterson & Peter Blood

Foreward by Harry Belafonte

Layout & Design by Annie Patterson

Appreciations

Deepest gratitude to Tinya Seeger for support and assistance, Joe Offer for research, assistance, & support, to Eleanor Warnock and Claire Brandenberg for proofing, and Paul Kaplan for his careful and skillful review of guitar chords. Thanks also to the many, many others who are helping to honor Pete and Toshi through carrying on their work for peace, justice and a sustainable planet.

All rights to Stormking Music, Inc., Sanga, Music, Inc. and Fall River Music, Inc. are administered by Figs. D Music c/o Concord Music Publishing. All rights to Kohaw Music, Inc. and Appleseed Music, Inc. are administered by Kohaw Music, Inc. c/o Concord Music Publishing. The arrangements of these publishers' songs in this book are © 2019. International Copyright Secured. All Rights Reserved. Reprinted by permission of Hal Leonard LLC.

Songs published by Ludlow Music Inc., Melody Trails Inc. and Folkways Music Publishers Inc. are administered by TRO Essex Music Group NA. All rights reserved. International copyrights secured. Used by permission.

All rights to other songs in this book are reserved to the original publisher listed under each song and are used by permission.

Unless otherwise noted, all quotations are by Pete Seeger from his autobiography, *Where Have All the Flowers Gone: A Singalong Memoir,* © 1993, 1997, 2009, used by permission of The Estate of Pete Seeger. The words written on the front cover drawing on Seeger's banjo head are a trademark of the Estate of Pete Seeger and are used by permission.

The quotation from Harry Belafonte spoken at SeegerFest in Manhattan is used by permission of Harry & Pamela Belafonte.

Quotation under "Which Side Are You On?" is by Philip S. Foner from the liner notes to the "Talking Union & Other Songs" album FW05285, courtesy of Smithsonian Folkways Recordings. (p) © 1955. Used by permission. This album can be purchased from Folkways as a CD. Information at https://folkways.si.edu.

© 2019 Anne Patterson and Peter Blood

ISBN # 978-1-5400-5630-6

www.groupsinging.org

Forward - by Harry Belafonte

The great reward for having lived 88 years is that for almost a century I was able to meet and to serve some of the greatest social activists and thinkers of our time.

None more exemplified the joy of that journey than did my friend Pete Seeger. It was another great figure, by the name of Paul Robeson, who said "artists are the gatekeepers of truth, they are civilizations' radical voice." For many of us, the embodiment of that observation could always be found in the humanity that Pete Seeger displayed in his every deed.

His courage was unflinching; his commitment to justice, irreversible. Knowing that there is inevitably a price to pay when speaking truth to power when facing the House Un-American Activities Committee, Pete understood "that although the House Un-American Activities Committee had the power to cage the singer, they did not have the power to cage the song."

Pete's song was sung for all of us. Through our hymns he introduced us to ourselves. "Wimoweh," the early call-out from an anguished black apartheid South Africa, to a most indifferent world, was heard by many of us for the first time, and Pete was its courier. When Pete and the Weavers sang it, we danced the hora: "Tzena, Tzena, Tzena," the joyous song of hope from young Jews in the Negev—only to be led to the tragic melodies of today sung by Shadia Mansour, and the Palestinian hymns of anguish for innocent children lying lifeless on the beaches of Gaza.

When last we spoke, "Where Have All the Flowers Gone" was on Pete's mind. We chatted about how could so much good that was on our horizon be so swiftly taken from us?

But for all the world's turmoil, Pete never blinked on the question as to whether or not our humanity had enough love in its power to triumph over our addiction to our inhumanity.

It was at Highlander, nestled in the mountains of Tennessee where first Martin Luther King, Jr. heard "We Shall Overcome." It was Pete who sang it to him and awakened the world to this slave song that became the anthem sung by a universe hungry for human dignity.

Pete made all of this his, made it his mission; but most of all he made the ending of our pain his common cause. And he was willing to settle—for, the only reward he would want would be the human triumph over evil. How long will it be before the space he once occupied be filled by another someone the human heart can trust?

Pete Seeger left us a legacy. He left it for every Native American languishing on the reservations in America, for every black man, woman and child, in the largest prison population in the world, for everyone hungry, for every refugee in the world.

Pete left us all attended to by his art and his incredible humanity.

- spoken by Harry Belafonte at SeegerFest in New York City in 2014

Singing Together

Pete believed passionately in community singing. He liked to say towards the end of his life that, if our world survives another hundred years, it could be in large part because of people singing with each other.

In 1985 we took a little homegrown singalong book to the board of *Sing Out! Magazine*. Pete and Toshi said: "We've got to put this out: This is what Sing Out is all about!" His manager Harold Leventhal got the big corporations to let us put in Beatles and Broadway songs. *Rise Up Singing* went on to sell hundreds of thousands of copies. What Pete loved most about it was that it had *so* many different kinds of songs in one songbook.

Pete Seeger was one of the great songleaders of our time. He got concert halls and even stadiums full of people all over the world singing along with him, often in languages they'd never even heard before. Pete used his singing as a way of reaching into the hearts of the people in his audiences and getting them to look at themselves, at people different from them, and at the world in fresh ways.

Let's continue building hope and changing the world by singing with each other.

- Annie Patterson & Peter Blood

Pete called his wife Toshi "the brains of the family." Toshi Seeger helped produce thousands of his concerts. She was a film-maker and producer. She co-directed his *Rainbow Quest* TV show, although her official credit was "Chief Cook & Bottle Washer." She was executive producer of the Emmy-winning documentary *Pete Seeger: The Power of Song.* They co-founded Clearwater (the environmental group dedicated to cleaning up the Hudson) and she played a central role in starting the Great Hudson River Revival, serving as its music director for many years.

After her death in July 2013, Pete expressed his love for his wife Toshi "without whom the world would not turn nor the sun shine." Pete died seven months later.

A Little a' This 'n' That

My grandma, she can make a soup
With a little a' this 'n' that
She can feed the whole sloop group
With a little a' this 'n' that
Stone soup! You know the story
Stone soup! Who needs the glory?
But with grandma cooking, no need to worry
Just **a little a' this 'n' that**

(up 3) Am D / Am - /   / E - / Am C / D F / Am E / Am -

Grandma likes to make a garden grow
With a little a' this 'n' that
But she likes to have the ground just so
With a little a' this 'n' that
Not too loose & not too firm
In the spring, the ground's all got to be turned
In the fall, lots of compost to feed the worms
With a little a' this 'n' that

Grandma knows we can build a future **with a little a'...**
And a few arguments never ever hurt ya **with a...**
True, this world's in a helluva fix
And some say oil & water don't mix
But they don't know a salad-maker's tricks **with...**

The world to come may be like a song **with...**
To make ev'rybody want to sing along **with...**
A little dissonance ain't no sin
A little skylarking to give us all a grin
Who knows but God's got a plan for the people to win
With a little a' this 'n' that

Pete Seeger (1991)

This song is Pete's homage to his wife Toshi Seeger's wisdom and genius as an organizer.

All Mixed Up

You know this language that we speak
Is part German, part Latin and part Greek
With some Celtic & Arabic all in a heap
_Well amended by the people in the street
   Choctaw gave us the word "okay"
   "Vamoose" is a word from Mexico way
   And all of this is a hint I suspect
   _Of what comes next

D G / A D :*//:* G D / A D :*//*

I think that this whole world
Soon, mama, my whole wide world
Soon, mama, my whole world
Soon gonna be get mixed up
  Soon, mama, my whole world
  Soon mama my whole wide world
  Soon mama my whole world
  Soon gonna be get mixed up

GD / D AD *//:* D GA / D AD :*//* (3x)

I like Polish sausage, I like Spanish rice
_Pizza pie is also nice
Corn & beans from the Indians here
Washed down by some German beer
   Marco Polo traveled by camel & pony
   _Brought to Italy, the first macaroni
   And you & I as well as we're able
   _Put it all on the table (I think that this…)

There were no red-headed Irishmen
Before the Vikings landed in Ireland
How many Romans had dark curly hair
Before they brought slaves from Africa?
    No race on earth is completely pure
    Nor is anyone's mind & that's for sure
    The winds mix the dust of every land
    And so will woman & man...

Oh this doesn't mean we must all be the same
We'll have different faces & different names
Long live many different kinds of races
And difference of opinion that makes horse races
    Just remember the rule about rules, brother
    What's right with one is wrong with another
    And take a tip from La Belle France:
    "Vive la difference!"

w: Pete Seeger (1960) m: Louise Bennett

© 1965 (renewed) by Stormking Music, Inc. Pete used this song as the opening to his autobiography, *Where Have All the Flowers Gone: A Singalong Memoir*. He believed that people borrowing and learning from others different from themselves will play a key role in the healing of our country - and our planet!

In trying to find ways we can work together, we'll use sports, arts, humor of many kinds. I've tried to combine old, old songs with brand new ones. Tried singing in different languages. Tried working with little kids, and with old folks. And above all urged folks to participate, in politics, in music, in all life. For example, there's this song I put together over 30 years ago. I swiped a Caribbean melody and a Caribbean beat.

Many Americans have found it easier to latch on to new traditions because we are uprooted people, and have few deep roots. But as compensation, we've often developed the ability to put down new roots very quickly. - P.S.

Banks of Marble

I've traveled 'round this country from shore to shining shore
It really made me wonder, the things I heard & saw

C - F C / F C G C

I saw the weary farmers plowing sod & loam
I heard the auction hammer just a-knockin' down their homes

But the banks are made of marble
With a guard at every door
And the vaults are stuffed with silver
That the <u>farmers</u> [*substitute:* seamen, miners, women] **sweated for**

C - / G C / - - / G C

I saw the seamen standing idly by the shore
I heard the bosses sayin' "Got no work for you no more"

I've seen the weary miners scrubbing coal dust from their backs
I heard their children crying "Got no coal to heat the shack"

I've seen my sisters working, on the job they're underpaid
While at home they work for nothing half the night & all the day

I've seen good people working throughout this mighty land
And I pray we'll get together & together make a stand

(final chorus) Then we'll own those banks of marble
With no guard at any door
And we'll share those vaults of silver
That we have sweated for!

Les Rice

The Bells Of Rhymney

"Oh what will you give me?" say the sad bells of Rhymney
"Is there hope for the future?" cry the brown bells of Merthyr
"Who made the mine owner?" say the black bells of Rhondda
"And who robbed the miner?" cry the grim bells of Blaina

(up 2) G - CG A G / G - FAm D / / 1st /

"They will plunder willy-nilly" cry the bells of Caerphilly
"They have fangs, they have teeth" shout the loud bells of Neath
"Even God is uneasy" say the moist bells of Swansea
"And what will you give me?" say the sad bells of Rhymney

"Throw the vandals in court," say the bells of Newport
"All will be well if, if, if..." cry the green bells of Cardiff
"Why so worried, sisters why?" sang the silver bells of Wye
"And what will you give me?" say the sad bells of Rhymney

G - CG A G / G Em FAm D / GF Em FEm G* / 1st /

(whistling tag) C G A - G - - / C G A - - G - - - -

*The Byrds played a "D" chord here

w: Idris Davies (1927) m: Pete Seeger (1959)

TRO © 1959, 1964 (renewed) Ludlow Music Inc. New York NY.
Davies was a Welsh coal miner, born in Rhymney. Later, he
was a school teacher & a friend of the poet Dylan Thomas.
Towns in verse 1 are in the impoverished coal mining
region of Wales. Those in verses 2 & 3 are more
prosperous towns. Cardiff is capital of Wales.

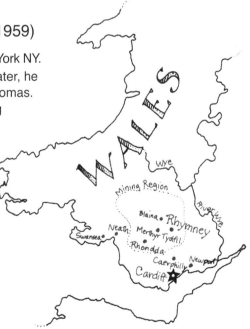

Bountiful River

Deep Love, like a Bountiful River,
    fills the soul, renews the heart
My love is always & ever, **we will never part**
Sailing, sailing together,
    fills the soul, renews the heart
Flowing, flowing forever, **we will never part**

**O Bountiful River, O Bountiful River
O Bountiful River, we will never part**

C Dm G C (repeat as needed)

Reviving, reviving this river **fills the soul, renews...**
Embarked on an endless endeavor, **we will never part**
Blending one voice with another **fills the soul, renews...**
Weaving our lives with these waters, **we will never part**

An eagle, circling in heaven, **fills the soul, renews...**
The eagle & river repeating, **we will never part**
Life giver, this Bountiful River **fills the soul, renews...**
Our spirits are mingled forever, **we will never part**

Our love for our sons & our daughters **fills the soul...**
Time now to care for these waters, **we will never part**

Pete Seeger & Lorre Wyatt

PETE'S THOUGHTS ON "BRING 'EM HOME" & SONGWRITING:
Not one of my best, this. An editorial in rhyme. I always caution beginning songwriters, "Beware of editorials in rhyme. Better: Tell a story." Nonetheless it did its job, got thousands singing that short refrain. And some life-long passions got into the verses. - P.S.

Bring 'Em Home

If you love this land of the free
   Bring 'em home, bring 'em home
Bring them back from overseas
   Bring 'em home, bring 'em home

(up 4) G - - - / Em - - - / C - G C / G D G -

It'll make the politicians sad, I know
   Bring 'em home, bring 'em home
They wanna tangle with their foe
   Bring 'em home, bring 'em home

They wanna test their grand theories...
With the blood of you & me...

We'll give no more brave young lives...
For the gleam in someone's eyes...

The men will cheer & the boys will shout...
And we will all turn out...

The church bells will ring with joy...
To welcome our darling girls & boys...

We'll will lift our voice in song...
When Johnny comes marching home…

Bring 'em home, bring 'em home (4x)

   Pete Seeger (1965)

ORIGINAL SEEGER CHORUS:

If you love your Uncle Sam / **Bring 'em home** (x2)
Support our boys in Vietnam / **Bring 'em home** (x2)

Deportee (Plane Wreck at Los Gatos)

The crops are all in & the peaches are rotting
The oranges are piled in their creosote dumps
They're flying you back to the Mexico border
To pay all your money to wade back again

Goodbye to my Juan, goodbye Rosalita
Adios mis amigos Jesús y Maria
You won't have a name when you ride the big airplane
All they will call you will be deportees

C FC / / F CAm / 1st // F C / G C / F C / C GC C

My father's own father, he waded that river
They took all the money he made in his life
My brothers & sisters come working the fruit trees
They rode the trucks 'til they took down & died
 Some of us are illegal & others are not wanted
 Our work contract's out & we have to move on
 600 miles to that Mexico border
 They chase us like outlaws, like rustlers, like thieves
We died in your hills, we died in your deserts
We died in your valleys & died on your plains
We died 'neath your trees & we died in your bushes
Both sides of the river, we died just the same
 The sky plane caught fire over Los Gatos canyon
 A fireball of lightning, it shook all our hills
 Who are these friends, all scattered like dry leaves?
 The radio says they are "just deportees"
Is this the best way we can grow our big orchards?
Is this the best way we can grow our good fruit?
To fall like dry leaves to rot on the topsoil
And be called by no name except deportee

w: poem by Woody Guthrie (1948)   m: Martin Hoffman (1958)

Woody Guthrie took Inspiration for "Deportee" from a *New York Times* article that omitted the names of migrant workers killed in a plane crash in 1948.

Get Up & Go

How do I know my youth is all spent?
My get up & go has got up & went
But in spite of it all, I'm able to grin
And think of the places my get up has been

(in A) D - A - / E - A - / D - A - / E - - A

Old age is golden, so I've heard said
But sometimes I wonder as I crawl into bed
With my ears in a drawer, my teeth in a cup
My eyes on the table until I wake up
    As sleep dims my vision, I say to myself
    Is there anything else I should lay on the shelf?
    But though nations are warring & business is vexed
    I'll stick around to see what happens next

A - E - / - - A - / D - A - / 1. B⁷ - - E :// 2. E - - A

When I was young, my slippers were red
I could kick up my heels right over my head
When I was older my slippers were blue
But still I could dance the whole night through
    Now I am older, my slippers are black
    I huff to the store & I puff my way back
    But never you laugh, I don't mind at all
    I'd rather be huffing than not puff at all

I get up each morning & dust off my wits
Open the paper & read the obits
If I'm not there, I know I'm not dead
So I eat a good breakfast & go back to bed

  w: collected, adapted & set to original music by Pete Seeger (1960)

God Bless the Grass

God bless the grass that grows through the crack
They roll the concrete over it to try & keep it back
The concrete gets tired of what it has to do
It breaks & it buckles & the grass grows through
And God bless the grass

Am - AmE Am / E - AmE Am / C Am C Am

F Am CD E - / Am E Am -

God bless the truth that fights toward the sun
They roll the lies over it & think that it is done
It moves through the ground & reaches for the air
And after a while it is growing everywhere and...

God bless the grass that grows through cement
It's green & it's tender & easily bent
But after a while it lifts up its head
For the grass is living & the stone is dead and...

God bless the grass that's gentle & low
Its roots they are deep & its will is to grow
And God bless the truth, the friend of the poor
And the wild grass growing at the poor man's door...

Malvina Reynolds

> *I met Malvina in the summer of 1947. I was 28 years old; she was 45, with beautiful white hair. She asked me if she could speak with me and give her some advice on getting started as a singer and a writer of songs. I make a practice of not discouraging people, but I confess when I first met her, I didn't perceive her genius. I think I had in the back of my mind a feeling, "Gosh, she's pretty old to get started as a musician." I had a lot to learn! - P.S.*

> *I've finally decided I have made my peace with the word "God." Most of my youth, thinking religion was the opiate of the people, I disliked using the word. But I found, like many other European-Americans, that I truly loved the religious songs of African-Americans. It was as though I rediscovered my own humanity through them. I knew Mahalia Jackson. She said, "I've seen God; I've seen the sun rise." I'm with you, Mahalia. I feel my heart lift every time I see the sun rise. Every time I see anything I feel I see God. - P.S.*

God's Counting on Me

When we l<u>oo</u>k & we see things are n<u>o</u>t what they should be
   God's counting on m<u>e</u>, God's counting on y<u>ou</u>
When we look & we see things are not what they should be
   God's counting on me, God's counting on you

(up 5) C - Am - / F G C - / 1st / Dm G C -

Hopin' we'll all pull through (3x) / **Me & you**
F G / CE Am / F G / C -

It's time to t<u>u</u>rn things around, trickle <u>u</u>p not trickle down
   God's counting on me, God's counting on you *(repeat)*

When drill baby drill leads to spill baby spill...

When there's big problems to be solved, let's get everyone involved...

Don't give up, don't give in, working together we all can win…

What we do now, you & me, will affect eternity…

When we work with younger folks, we can never give up hope...

When push comes to shove, may-be the remedy is love...

Pete Seeger & Lorre Wyatt

Goodnight Irene

Irene goodnight (2x)
Goodnight Irene, goodnight Irene
I'll see you in my dreams

D - A - / - - D - / D D7 G - / A - D -

Sometimes I live in the country
Sometimes I live in town
Sometimes I take a great notion
To jump into the river & drown

Stop your ramblin', stop your gamblin'
Stop staying out late at night
Go home to your wife & family
Stay there by the fireside bright

You cause me to weep, you cause to mourn
You cause me to leave my home
But the very last words I heard her say
Was "Please sing me one more song"

Huddie ("Leadbelly") Ledbetter & John Lomax

TRO © 1936 & 1950 (renewed) Ludlow Music Inc., New York NY. The Weavers' recording of this song reached #1 on the hit parade in 1950, shortly before they were blacklisted from the airwaves & from most commercial venues for their left-wing associations. For more verses see *Rise Up Singing*.

The origins of "Guantanamera"

José Marti was a Cuban poet exiled to NYC for 12 years for his independence work. In 1895 he returned to Cuba and was killed in an abortive uprising. The verses of "Guantanamera" are from a long poem, *Versos Sencillos* - Marti's last book.

Popular singer José Fernandez Diaz ("Joseito") composed this song in the 1920's satirizing Cuban women living near Guantanamo naval base who dated U.S. sailors based there. He had a radio show in the 1940's and would make up new verses to his song based on the news of the day. Julian Orbon was a classical pianist who discovered you could put verses from Marti's poem to Joseito's song.

Héctor Angulo, a student of Orbon's studying music in NYC, got a job at Camp Woodland, a camp in the Catskills which Pete often visited. During his visit in 1962 the campers insisted that Pete listen to the "great song our counselor is teaching us". Pete taught it to the Weavers and wanted Americans to sing it during the 1963 Cuban missile crisis as a way of showing solidarity with Cuba.

Guantanamera

Guantanamera, guajira / Guantanamera *(repeat)*

(in D) G - A - / D Em A - /   /   /

Yo soy un hombre sincero
De donde crece la palma *(repeat)*
Y antes de morirme quiero
Echar mis versos del alma

D Em A - (6x)

Mi verso es de un verde claro
Y de un carmín encendido *(repeat)*
Mi verso es un ciervo herido
Que busca en el monte amparo

Con los pobres de la tierra
Quiero yo mi suerte echar *(repeat)*
Y el arroyo de la sierra
Me complace más que el mar

Cultivo la rosa blanca
En junio, como en enero *(repeat)*
Para el amigo sincero
Que me da su mano franca

Y para el cruel que me arranca
El corazón con que vivo *(repeat)*
Cardo ni ortiga cultivo
Cultivo la rosa blanca

Music adap. by Pete Seeger & Julian Orbon. Lyric adaptation by Julian Orbon,
based on a poem by José Marti. Lyric editor Hector Angulo.
Original music & lyrics by José Fernandez Diaz

I cultivate a white rose in June & in January
For the sincere friend who gives me his hand.
And for the cruel one who would tear out this heart with which I live
I cultivate neither thistles nor nettles - I cultivate a white rose.

Healing River

O healing river, send down your water
Send down your water upon this land
O healing river, send down your water
And wash the blood from off the sand

GC GD (x2) / G A DA D

GC GB7 Em A / GEm AmD G(C GD)

This land is parching, this land is thirsting
No seed is growing on the barren ground
O healing river, send down your water
O healing river, send your water down

as above but line 4: GEm AmD G (C GB⁷)

(bridge) O seed of freedom, awake & flourish
Let the deep roots nourish, let the tall stalks rise
O seed of freedom, awake & flourish
Proud leaves unfurling unto the sky   *(repeat 1st verse)*

Em - B⁷ - / Em - EmA DA D /

GC GB⁷ Em A / GEm AmD G(C GD)

Fred Hellerman & Fran Minkoff

Pete worked with Mississippi Freedom Summer in 1964. While he was singing with a group one night he was passed a note that the bodies of the three civil rights workers murdered by the Klan a month earlier had finally been discovered. After passing along this sad news to those present, Pete sang "Healing River".
He wrote the song "Those Three Are on My Mind" the next year.

Hobo's Lullaby

Go to sleep, you weary hobo
Let the towns drift slowly by
Can't you hear the steel rails humming
That's the hobo's lullaby

D G / A D :∥

I know your clothes are torn & ragged
And your hair is turning gray
Lift your head & smile at trouble
You'll find peace & rest someday

Don't you worry 'bout tomorrow
Let tomorrow come & go
Tonight you're in a nice warm boxcar
Safe from all that wind & snow

I know the police cause you trouble
They cause trouble everywhere
But when you die & go to Heaven
There'll be no policemen there

Goebel Reeves

I was at a board meeting of Sing Out in Kansas City. As we were finishing lunch, I asked Pete casually to tell me about when he first met Woody Guthrie. He launched into a wondrous two-hour recounting of traveling around this country with Woody in 1939, hitch-hiking, riding the rails. Pete skinned his knees and broke his banjo the first time he jumped a freight train with Woody. They visited and sang with workers on picket lines, left-wing organizers, migrants, hobos. If only I had had a tape recorder! Woody mentored Seeger as a budding musician-activist, just as Pete later mentored countless others. (Pete later asked me to edit his autobiography, *Where Have All the Flowers Gone: A Singalong Memoir.*) - Peter Blood

How Can I keep from Singing

My life flows on in endless song
Above earth's lamentation
I hear the real, though far-off hymn
That hails a new creation
Through all the tumult & the strife
I hear the music ringing
It sounds an echo in my soul
How can I keep from singing?

D G / D A / 1st / DA D / - - /   / D GD / DA D

What though the tempest 'round me roars
I hear the truth, it liveth
What though the darkness 'round me close
Songs in the night it giveth
No storm can shake my inmost calm
While to that rock I'm clinging
Since love is lord of heaven & earth
How can I keep from singing?

When tyrants tremble, sick with fear
And hear their death-knells ringing
When friends rejoice, both far & near
How can I keep from singing?
In prison cell & dungeon vile
Our thoughts to them are winging
When friends by shame are undefiled
How can I keep from singing?

orig. w: unknown, verse 3 Doris Plenn, lyrics adap. by Pete Seeger
m: Rev. Robert Lowry (1826-1899)

If I Had a Hammer

If I had a hammer, I'd hammer in the morning
I'd hammer in the evening, all over this land
I'd hammer out danger, I'd hammer out a warning
I'd hammer out love between my brothers & my sisters
All over this land

C Em F G (x2) / C Em F - G - - - /
C - - - Am - - - / F C F C / F C G - C Em F G (x2)

If I had a bell, I'd ring it in the morning
I'd ring out danger...warning...

If I had a song, I'd sing it in the morning...

Well, I've got a hammer & I've got a bell
And I've got a song to sing all over this land
It's the hammer of justice, it's the bell of freedom
It's a song about love between my brothers & my sisters
All over this land

(tag): It's a hammer of justice, it's a bell of freedom
It's a song about love between my brothers & my sisters
All over this land

C - - - Am - - - / F C F C / F C G - C - G - C - - -

Words: Lee Hays music: Pete Seeger (1949)

TRO © 1958 (renewed) & 1962 (renewed) Ludlow Music Inc. New York NY. When they wrote this
song they had no idea how popular it would eventually become. These chords are new ones from
Peter, Paul & Mary. The original line was "love between all of my brothers". Pete learned the more
inclusive language from Libby Frank & eventually was able to persuade Lee to sing it that way.

*I often sing "The Water Is Wide" right after a gang has raised the roof on
"If I Had a Hammer" saying: "All our militance, enthusiasm, bravery will
count for nothing if we can't cross the oceans of misunderstanding between
the peoples of this world…"   - P.S.*

Joe Hill

I dreamed I saw Joe Hill last night
Alive as you & me
Says I "But Joe, you're ten years dead"
"I never died" says he (2x)

A - / D A / D EA / B⁷ E / - A

"In Salt Lake, Joe, by God" says I
Him standing by my bed
"They framed you on a murder charge"
Says Joe "But I ain't dead" (2x)

"The copper bosses killed you, Joe
They shot you, Joe" says I
"Takes more than guns to kill a man"
Says Joe "I didn't die" (2x)

And standing there as big as life
Smiling with his eyes
Joe says "What they forgot to kill
Went on to organize" (2x)

From San Diego up to Maine
In every mine & mill
Where workers strike & organize
It's there you'll find Joe Hill (2x)

w: Alfred Hayes m: Earl Robinson

Joe Hill was a Swedish immigrant and labor activist. He was a member of the Industrial Workers of the World (the IWW or "Wobblies"). Hill wrote many well-known songs including "There Is Power in the Union", "The Rebel Girl" and "The Preacher & the Slave" ("Pie in the Sky"). He was arrested and convicted for allegedly killing a man in a grocery store robbery. He was executed by firing squad in Utah in 1915 despite international appeals for clemency including from Woodrow Wilson and Helen Keller. Most believe today that he was innocent and essentially executed for his political activism.

Kisses Sweeter than Wine

When I was a young man & never been kissed
I got to thinking over what I had missed
I got me a girl, I kissed her & then
Oh Lord - I kissed her again
Oh, kisses sweeter than wine (2x)

D⁹

F C Dm C / Am - Dm - :///: F - Am / Dm C D⁹ - ://

I asked her to marry & be my sweet wife
And we would be so happy the rest of our lives
I begged & I pleaded like a natural man
And then, oh Lord - she gave me her hand

I worked mighty hard & so did my wife
Workin' hand in hand to make a good life
With corn in the field & wheat in the bins
I was, oh Lord - the father of twins

Our children numbered just about four
They all had sweethearts knockin' on the door
They all got married & they didn't hesitate
I was, oh Lord - the grandfather of eight

Now we are old & ready to go
We get to thinkin' what happened a long time ago
We had a lot of kids, trouble & pain
But, oh Lord - we'd do it again

w: Ronnie Gilbert, Lee Hays, Fred Hellerman & Pete Seeger (1950)
m: Huddie ("Leadbelly") Ledbetter

Let's sing it for all those who never had any children but who left us things we use: the word-makers, the picture makers, the inventors of things and recipes, the bridgemakers, the liberators, the peacemakers.
- P.S.

Last Night I Had the Strangest Dream

Last night I had the strangest dream
I never dreamed before
I dreamed the world had all agreed
To put an end to war

C - - - / F - C - / G - C Am / Dm G C -

I dreamed I saw a mighty room
Filled with women & men
And the paper they were signing said
They'd never fight again

F - C - / G - C - :||

And when the paper was all signed
And a million copies made
They all joined hands & bowed their heads
And grateful prayers were prayed

And the people in the streets below
Were dancing round & round
And swords & guns & uniforms
Were scattered on the ground   *(repeat 1st verse)*

Ed McCurdy

TRO © 1950, 1951, 1953 (renewed) Folkways Music Publishers Inc. New York NY. McCurdy had a wide ranging career as a romantic singer, comedian, TV host and later as a folksinger. His song has been recorded in over 75 languages. You can view children singing this song on the East Berlin wall during TV coverage of the dismantling of the Berlin Wall.

If you are leading "Letter to Eve" with folks who don't know it well, take time to teach 'em the last line. The first "pacem in terris" is Latin. "Mir" - that's Russian for peace. "Shanti" - 800 million people in India would understand that. "Salaam" - that's known not only in the mid-East, most of Africa know it too. Indonesia & Pakistan as well. "Heiwa" is the Japanese way of pronouncing two Chinese characters that mean the same thing: peace in the world. - P.S.

Letter to Eve

Oh Eve, where is Adam, now you're kicked out of the garden? (2x)
Been wanderin' from shore to shore, now you find that there's
no more

Oh-oh pacem in terris, mir, shanti, salaam, heiwa!

(up 3) Am - - - / - - - E / Am Am⁷ D⁷ F / Am ↓ FE Am -

Don't you wish love, only love, could save this world from disaster? (2x)
Don't you wish love could end the confusion or is it just one
more illusion?

If you want to have great love, you've got to have great anger (2x)
When I see innocent folks shot down, you want me to just
shake my head & frown

If you want to hit the target square, you better not have blind anger (2x)
Or else it'll just be one more time, the correction creates
another crime!

If music could only bring peace, I'd only be a musician (2x)
If songs could do more than dull the pain, if melodies could
only break these chains!

Oh Eve, you tell Adam, next time he asks you / Yes Eve...
He'll say "Baby it's cold outside, what's the password to come
inside?" / You say: "Oh pacem in terris…"

Oh Eve, go tell Adam, we've got to build a new garden (2x)
We got to get working on the building of a decent home for all
of God's children!

Oh-oh pacem in terris, mir, shanti, salaam, heiwa! (2x)
4000 languages in this world, means the same thing to every
boy & girl

Pete Seeger (1967)

© 1967 (renewed) Sanga Music, Inc. Pete wrote that this song, inspired by Genesis, was orig. meant to be a dialogue between a pacifist and a freedom fighter. Then it changed to be more a song for women.

Lonesome Valley

You got to walk that lonesome valley
You got to walk it by yourself
Nobody here can walk it for you
You got to walk it by yourself

D G D - / A - D - / G - D - / D A D -

Now, Daniel was a Bible hero
He was a prophet brave & true
In a den of hungry lions
He proved what faith can do for you.

Some folks say John was a Baptist
Some folks say he was a Jew
But the Holy Bible tells us
That he was a preacher too.

Now though the road be rough & rocky
And the hills be steep & high
We can sing as we go marching
And we'll win that one big union by & by!

new words & new music adaptation by Woody Guthrie

In his own way Woody was very religious. When he went into a hospital in 1952, he said intently to us, "Only God can help me."
When a nurse asked him what religion he was so she could fill out a form, he replied, "All." She asked him again and said he must give one or another. His reply was, "All or none." - P.S.

22

Midnight Special

Yonder come Miss Rosie, how in the world do you know?
I know her by her apron & the dress she wore
Umbrella on her shoulder, piece of paper in her hand
She goes a marchin' to the governor "Turn loose my man!"

(in D) G - - - / D - - - / A - - - / D - ://

Oh let the Midnight Special shine her light on me
Let the Midnight Special shine her ever lovin' light on me

G - - - D - - - / A - - - - *(there's an extra beat!)* D - - -

If you ever go to Houston, oh you better walk right
And you better not stagger & you better not fight
Sheriff Benson will arrest you, he'll take you down
You can bet your bottom dollar: you're penitentiary bound

Now you wake up in the morning, hear the ding dong ring
You go a marching to the table, you see the same damn thing
Knife & fork are on the table, & nothin' in my pan
And if you say a thing about it, you're in trouble with the "man"

Now here comes jumpin' Judy, I'll tell you how I know
You know, Judy brought jumpin' to the whole wide world
She brought it in the morning about the break of day
You know, if I ever get to jumpin' - oh Lord I'll up & jump away

Well Huddie Ledbetter he was a mighty fine man
Huddie taught us this song & to the whole wide land
Now he's done with all his grieving, whooping hollerin' & a-cryin'
Now he's done with all his studying about his great long time

new words & new music adaptation by Huddie ("Leadbelly") Ledbetter
collected by John A. Lomax & Alan Lomax, final verse by Pete Seeger

23

Of Time & Rivers Flowing

Of time & rivers flowing, the seasons make a song
And we who live beside her still try to sing along
Of rivers, fish & men, & the season still a-coming
When she'll run clear again
La la la... *(to tune of 1st 2 lines)*
Of rivers, fish & men, & the season still a-coming
When she'll run clear again

C Am DmG C /   / GD G - CF Am / DmG C ://

So many homeless sailors, so many winds that blow
I asked the half-blind scholars which way the currents flow
So cast your nets below & the gods of moving waters
Will tell us all they know
La la la... So cast your nets below...*(repeating last 2 lines of verse)*

The circles of the planets, the circles of the moon
The circles of the atoms all play a marching tune
And we who would join in can stand aside no longer
Now let us all begin!
La la la... And we who would join in... *(last 2 lines of verse)*

Pete Seeger (1973)

Oh Had I a Golden Thread

Oh, had I a golden thread
And needle so fine
I'd weave a magic strand
Of rainbow design (2x)

(capo up) D - G - / D - A - :// G DA D -

In it I'd weave the bravery
Of women giving birth
In it I'd weave the innocence
Of children over all the earth
Children of all earth

Far over the waters
I'd reach my magic band
Through foreign cities
To every single land
To every land

Show my brothers & sisters
My rainbow design
Bind up this sorry world
With hand & heart & mind
Hand & heart & mind

Far over the waters
I'd reach my magic band
To every human being
So they would understand
So they'd understand   *(repeat 1st verse)*

Pete Seeger (1958)

Old Devil Time

Old Devil Time, I'm gonna fool you now!
Old Devil Time, you'd like to bring me down!
When I'm feeling low, **my lovers gather 'round**
And help me rise to fight you one more time!

C D G - / CD G D - / 1st / C D G (CD G -)

Old Devil Fear, you with your icy hands
Old Devil Fear, you'd like to freeze me cold!
But when I'm sore afraid, **my lovers gather 'round**
And help me rise to fight you one more time!

Old Devil Pain, you often pinned me down
You thought I'd cry & beg you for the end
But at that very time, **my lovers gather 'round**
And help me rise to fight you one more time!

Old Devil Hate, I knew you long ago
Then I found out the poison in your breath
Now when we hear your lies, **my lovers gather 'round**
And help me rise to fight you one more time!

No storm or fire can ever beat us down
No wind that blows but carries us further on
And you who fear, <u>oh</u> lovers, gather 'round
And we can rise & sing it one more time!

Pete Seeger (1969)

Written for the Otto Preminger film "Tell Me that You Love Me, Junie Moon" starring Liza Minnelli.

Old Time Religion

Give me that old time religion (3x)
That's good enough for me

(up 2) D - / A D / - G / DA D

We will pray with Aphrodite
Even tho' she's rather flighty
She wears that see-through nightie
And that's good enough for me

We will pray with those Egyptians
Build pyramids to put our crypts in
Cover subways with inscriptions...

Let me follow dear old Buddha
There is nobody cuta
He comes in plastic, wood or pewta...

We will pray with Zarathustra
We'll pray just like we use ta
I'm a Zarathustra boosta...

We will pray with those old Druids
They drink fermented fluids
Waltzing naked thru the woo-ids...

Hare Krishna gets a laugh on
When he sees me dressed in saffron
With my hair that's only half on...

I'll arise at early morning
When my Lord gives me the warning
That the solar age is dawning...

verses: anonymous "filksong", final verse by Pete Seeger (1982)
chorus & tune: traditional gospel hymn

Precious Friend

Just when I thought / All was lost, you changed my mind
You gave me hope (not just the old soft soap)
You showed that we could learn to share in time
   (you & me & Rockefeller)

G D⁷Eb⁷ G - / C - G - / G D⁷Eb⁷ G Em / A⁷ - D -

I'll keep pluggin' on
Your face will shine through all our tears
And when we sing another little victory song
Precious friend, you will be there, singing in harmony
Precious friend, you will be there

G D⁷Eb⁷ G - / C - B⁷ - /
C A⁷ G E⁷ / A⁷ D⁷ G E⁷ / A⁷ D⁷ GC G

  Pete Seeger (1974)

Quite Early Morning

Don't you know it's darkest before the dawn
And this thought keeps me moving on
If we could heed these early warnings
The time is now quite early morning *(repeat last 2 lines)*

(in D) A D / //: G D / A D ://

Some say that humankind won't long endure
But what makes them so doggone sure?
I know that you who hear my singing
Could make those freedom bells go ringing / I know that...

And so we keep on while we live
Until we have no, no more to give
And when these fingers can strum no longer
Hand the old banjo to young ones stronger / And when…

So though it's darkest before the dawn
These thoughts keep us moving on
Through all this world of joy & sorrow
We still can have singing tomorrows / Through all this world…

Pete Seeger (1969)

Rainbow Race

One blue sky above us
One ocean lapping all our shores
One earth so green & round
Who could ask for more?
And because I love you
I'll give it one more try
To show my rainbow race
It's too soon to die

G Am / D G / E⁷ Am / D G :∥

Some folks want to be like an ostrich
Bury their heads in the sand
Some hope that plastic dreams
Can unclench all those greedy hands
Some want to take the easy way
Poisons, bombs, they think we need them
Don't you know you can't kill all the unbelievers
There's no shortcut to freedom

Go tell, go tell all the little children
Tell all the mothers & fathers too
Now's our last chance to learn to share
What's been given to me & you

Pete Seeger (1967)

Sailing Down My Golden River

Sailing down my golden river
Sun & water all my own
  Yet I was never alone
Sun & water, old life givers
I'll have them where e'er I roam
  And I was not far from home

D Bm Em A / D EmA D - ://

Sunlight glancing on the water
Life & death are all my own
  Yet I was never alone
Life to raise my sons & daughters
Golden sparkles in the foam
  And I was not far from home

Sailing down this winding highway
Travelers from near and far
  Yet I was never alone
Exploring all the little byways
Sighting all the distant stars
  And I was not far from home

Pete Seeger (1962)

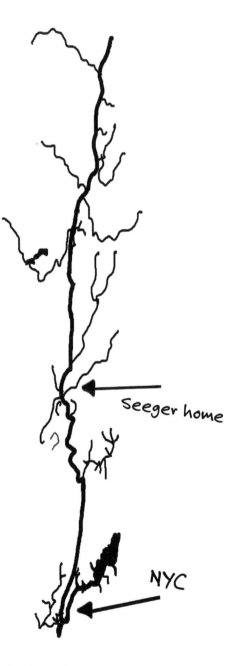

Seeger home

NYC

Map of the Hudson River

Sailing Up My Dirty Stream

Sailing up my dirty stream
Still I love it & I'll keep the dream
That some day, though maybe not this year
My Hudson River will once again run clear

G - - - / Am⁷ D G - / 1st / Am⁷ D⁷ G -

> She starts high in the mountains of the north
> Crystal clear & icy trickles forth
> With just a few floating wrappers of chewing gum
> Dropped by some hikers to warn of things to come

G↓ - - / Am⁷ - D - / 1st / Am⁷ D⁷ G -

At Glens Falls 5000 honest hands
Work at the Consolidated Paper Plant
Five million gallons of waste a day
Why should we do it any other way?

> Down the valley one million toilet chains
> Find my Hudson so convenient a place to drain
> And each little city says "Who, me?
> Do you think that sewage plants come free?"

Out in the ocean they say the water's clear
But I live right at Beacon here
Halfway between the mountains & the sea
Tacking to & fro, this thought returns to me:

> Sailing up my dirty stream
> Still I love it & I'll keep the dream
> That some day, though maybe not this year
> My Hudson River & my country will run clear!

Pete Seeger (1961)

The Hudson river *does*, in fact, run far clearer than when Pete & Toshi founded Clearwater in 1966.
The day when our country runs clear is going to take a little longer...

Sailing Up, Sailing Down

Sailing up (sailing up), Sailing down (sailing down)
Up (down), Down (up!) - **up & down the river**
Sailing on, stopping all along the way
The river may be dirty now,
   but she's getting cleaner every day

C - / - - / F - C - / G F C (G)

People come (people come), People go (people go)
Come (go!), Go (come!) - **up & down the river**
Sailing on, stopping all along the way
The river may be dirty now, but she's getting...

Garbage here (garbage here), Garbage there (garbage there)
Here (there!), There (here!) - **up & down the river...**

Catching fish (catching fish), Catching hell (catching hell)
Fish (hell!), Hell (fish!) - **up & down the river...**

Singing here (singing here), Singing there (singing there)
Here (there!), There (here!) - **up & down the river...**

Lorre Wyatt

In 1962 Rachel Carson's book Silent Spring made a turning point in my life. As a kid I'd been a nature nut. At age 15 and 16 I put all that behind me, figuring the main job to do was to help the meek inherit the earth, assuming that when they did the foolishness of the private profit system would be put to an end.

But in the early '60's I realized that the world was being turned into a poisonous garbage dump. By time the meek inherited it, it might not be worth inheriting. - P.S

Step by Step

Step by step the longest march
Can be won, can be won
Many stones can form an arch
Singly none, singly none
    And by union what we will
    Can be accomplished still
    Drops of water turn a mill
    Singly none, singly none

Dm - - - / Gm Dm Gm Dm *:∥*

Dm - - - / Dm Gm - A / Dm Gm - Dm / Gm Dm Gm Dm

lyrics adapted from The American Mineworkers Assoc. Constitution (1870)
music adapted from a traditional Irish folk song
arranged & adapted by Waldemar Hille & Pete Seeger (1948)

© 1991 Sanga Music, Inc. These lyrics are taken almost word for word from the preamble to the constitution of the first miners' union in the U.S. *People's Songs* bulletin was the predecessor of *Sing Out! Magazine*, which was founded by Pete in 1950. "Step by Step" is the title song of a recording by Annie Patterson & Charlie King. In just a few words, this song tells us what unions stand for.

Waldemar Hille, editing the People's Songs *bulletin* in 1948, once showed me two short verses he found when researching U.S. labor history. It was printed in the preamble to the constitution of an early coal miners' union.*

Says Wally, "Good verse." Says I, "What's the tune?" "I don't know," says Wally, "I suppose some old Irish tune might fit it. Like the song from the Irish famine of the 1840's, 'The Praties They Grow Small.'"

"Let's try it," says I. It fit. And has been sung to that melody ever since.
  - P.S.

This Land Is Your Land

This land is your land, this land is my land
From California to the New York island
From the redwood forest to the Gulf Stream waters
This land was made for you & me

G - D - / A - D - ://

As I went walking that ribbon of highway
I saw above me that endless skyway
I saw below me that golden valley
This land was made for you & me

I've roamed and rambled & I followed my footsteps
To the sparkling sands of her diamond deserts
While all around me a voice was sounding…

Well the sun came shining & I was strolling
And the wheat fields waving & the dust clouds rolling
As the fog was lifting, a voice was chanting…

Was a great high wall there that tried to stop me
Was a great big sign there said "Private Property"
But on the other side, it didn't say nothing / That side was…

In the squares of the city in the shadow of a steeple
By the relief office I saw my people
As they stood there hungry, I stood there asking
Is this land made for you & me?

Nobody living can ever stop me
As I go walking that freedom highway
Nobody living can ever make me turn back…

Woody Guthrie (1940)

Those Three Are on My Mind

I think of Andy in the cold wet clay
Those three are on my mind
With his friends beside him on that brutal day
Those three are on my mind

C ↓ - - / F G C - ://

There lies young James in his mortal pain...
While my tears keep falling like the rain, like the rain...

I see young Michael with his soft-eyed bride...
And three proud mothers weeping side by side...

> But I breathe yet & for some the sky is bright
> I cannot give up hoping for a morning light
> So I ask the killers "Can you sleep at night?"
> **Those three are on my mind** (2x)
>
> F - C - / / F G C Am /   / F G C -

I see the tin-roofed shanties where my people live...
And the burnt-out churches where they sing "we forgive"...

> While on the backwoods roads still ride the hooded bands
> Poisoning the air through the good southlands
> And so I ask the killers "Can you ever wash your hands?"
> **Those three are on...** (2x)

There sit the mighty judges handing down the law...
In their marble courthouse we are filled with awe...

> I know Tom Paine's watered tree, I know the price of liberty
> But I must ask the question that burns inside of me:
> Did they also murder justice when they killed those three?...

w: Frances Taylor m: Pete Seeger (1965)

35

To Everyone in All the World

To everyone in all the world
I reach my hand, I shake their hand
To everyone in all the world
I shake their hands like this

D - / A D :‖

All, all together
The whole wide world around
I may not know your lingo
But I can say "By jingo!"
No matter where you live we can shake hands

G D / A D / G D / / G DA D -

À tous et chacun dans le monde
Je tends la main, j' leur donne la main
À tous et chacun dans le monde
Je donne la main comme ça

Tous, tous ensemble
Au monde entier je chante
C'est très facile entre humains
Avec une poignée de main
N'importe où dans le monde on peut s'entendre

Pete Seeger (1956), with additional French lyrics by Raffi

To My Old Brown Earth

To my old brown earth & to my old blue sky
I'll now give these last few molecules of "I"
And you who sing & you who stand nearby
I do charge you not to cry

CF C CDm C / Dm G CG C

CF C CDm C / F C Am -

Guard well our human chain,
    watch well you keep it strong
As long as sun will shine
And this our home keep
    pure & sweet & green
For now I'm yours & you are also mine

GF G GF G / Dm - G -

CF C CDm C / Dm G Dm G C -

Pete Seeger (1958)

© 1958 (renewed) by Stormking Music, Inc.

> *In 1958 I sang at the funeral of John McManus,*
> *co-editor of the radical newsweekly,* The Guardian,
> *and regretted that I had no song worthy of the*
> *occasion. So this got written. I send it to the family*
> *of someone who has died - with a hand-colored*
> *flower alongside it.   - P.S.*

Turn! Turn! Turn!

To everything - turn, turn, turn
There is a season - turn, turn, turn
And a time to every purpose under heaven

(up 2) G C G Am - /   / D - - - / G - - -

A time to be born, a time to die
A time to plant, a time to reap
A time to kill, a time to heal
A time to laugh, a time to weep

D - G - (3x) C D G - -

A time to build up, a time to break down
A time to dance, a time to mourn
A time to cast away stones /A time to gather stones together

A time of love, a time of hate /A time of war, a time of peace
A time you may embrace /A time to refrain from embracing

A time to gain, a time to lose /A time to rend, a time to sew
A time of love, a time of hate /A time of peace, I swear it's not too late

w: Ecclesiastes 3:1-8 music & adapted lyrics: Pete Seeger (1954)

TRO © 1962 (renewed) Melody Trails Inc. New York NY. Recorded by the Byrds in 1965.

Tzena Tzena

Tzena (x4 - 2nd verse x2 only) habanot, urena
Chayalim bamoshava
Al-na (x4 - 2nd verse x2 only) al-na titchabena
Miben-chayil ish tzava *(repeat stanza with different melody)*

A - D - / E - A - :‖

Tzena (x2) *(clap)* tzena (x3)
Tzena (x2) tzena (x4) *(repeat)*

A - D - / E - - - / A - D - / E - - A

Lyrics in Arabic (by Salman Natour):

Zeina (x4) dabkeh nihdbek nurkus hora
Bleilet twa adna
Yalla ma'ana, rudu ma'ana (x3)
Ghrannu ya ah-bab

Zeina, zeina, dabkeh nihdbek yalla
Nurkus hora ya as-ha-a-a-ab.
Yalla ma'ana, yalla rudu ma'ana
Ah-lan bikom ya as-hab!

Zeina zeina *(clap)* zeina zeina zeina...

Lyrics in English (per Weavers, adapted by Pete Seeger):

Tzena (x4) can't you hear the music playing
In the city square?
Tzena (x4) come where all our friends will find us
With the dancers there

Tzena (x2) join the celebration
There'll be people there from ev'ry nation
Dawn will find us laughing in the sunlight
Dancing in the city square

Tzena (x2) come & dance the hora
Dance the dabke, sing with me we'll dance together
Tzena (x2) when the band is playing
My heart's saying "Tzena tzena tzena!"

Hebrew lyrics by Yehiel Haggiz (1941), music by Issachar Miron
English lyrics Mitchell Parish & Pete Seeger

"Tzena Tzena" was composed in Israel in 1941. It was recorded by The Weavers in 1950 as the "B" side of their hit recording "Goodnight Irene". Pete was deely concerned about the Palestinian-Israeli conflict. He chose to include in the 2009 edition of his autobiography these singable Arabic lyrics. Pete also slightly altered the English lyrics to emphasize the message of peace. The dabke is an Arabic folk dance often danced by Palestinians as well as other Arabic groups in the region.

Union Maid

There once was a union maid who never was afraid
Of goons & ginks & company finks
And the deputy sheriffs who made the raid
She went to the union hall when a meeting it was called
And when the company boys came 'round
She always stood her ground

C - F C / F C / D7 G / 1st / F C / G C

Oh you can't scare me, I'm sticking to the union
I'm sticking to the union (x2)
Oh you can't scare me, I'm sticking to the union
I'm sticking to the union 'til the day I die

F - C - / G - C - ://

This union maid was wise to the tricks of company spies
She couldn't be fooled by a company stool
She'd always organize the guys
She'd always get her way when she struck for better pay
She'd show her card to the National Guard
And this is what she'd say:

You women who want to be free, take a little tip from me
Break outa that mold that we've all been sold:
You've got a fighting history!
The fight for women's rights with workers must unite
Like Mother Jones, move those bones
To the front of every fight!

Woody Guthrie

Viva la Quince Brigada

Viva la quince brigada - **rúmbala, rúmbala, rúmbala** (2x)
Que se ha cubierto de gloria - **ay Manuela, ay Manuela** (2x)

Am - E - /   / Am AmG GF FE E /   /

Luchamos contra los moros - **rúmbala, rúmbala, rúmbala** (2x)
Mercenarios y fascistas - **ay Manuela, ay Manuela** (2x)

Solo es nuestro deseo - **rúmbala, rúmbala, rúmbala** (2x)
Acabar con el fascismo - **ay Manuela, ay Manuela** (2x)

En el frente de Jarama - **rúmbala, rúmbala, rúmbala** (2x)
No tenemos ni aviones, ni tanques ni cañones - ay Manuela (2x)

Ya salimos de España - **rúmbala, rúmbala, rúmbala** (2x)
Por luchar en otros frentes - **ay Manuela, ay Manuela** (2x)

Traditional folk song. Adapted by Bart Van Der Scheling

Spain 1937. Long live the Fifteenth Brigade. We fought against the Moors. We fought against the mercenaries & the fascists. It was our only desire to defeat fascism. But on the Jarama Front we had no tanks, no cannon, no airplanes. Then the last verse says: Now we are leaving Spain, but we'll keep on fighting on other fronts. - P.S.

Waist Deep in the Big Muddy

It was back in 1942
I was a member of a good platoon
We were on maneuvers in Loozianna
One night by the light of the moon
The captain told us to ford a river
That's how it all begun
We were knee deep in the Big Muddy
But the big fool said to push on

(up 3) Am ↓ AmE Am / Am ↓ Dm E /   / Am - E Am

The Sergeant said "Sir, are you sure
This is the best way back to the base?"
"Sergeant, go on! I forded this river
'Bout a mile above this place
It'll be a little soggy but just keep slogging
We'll soon be on dry ground"
We were waist deep in the Big Muddy
And the big fool said to push on

> Well, the Sergeant said "Sir, with all this equipment
> No man will be able to swim"
> "Sergeant, don't be a Nervous Nellie"
> The captain said to him
> "All we need is a little determination
> Men, follow me, I'll lead on"
> We were neck deep in the Big Muddy
> And the big fool said to push on

All at once, the moon clouded over
We heard a gurgling cry
A few seconds later, the captain's helmet
Was all that floated by
The Sergeant said, "Turn around men
I'm in charge from now on"
And we just made it out of the Big Muddy
With the captain dead & gone

We stripped & dived & found his body
Stuck in the old quicksand
I guess he didn't know that the water was deeper
Than the place he'd once before been
Another stream had joined the Big Muddy
'Bout a half mile from where we'd gone
We were lucky to escape from the Big Muddy
When the big fool said to push on

 Well I'm not going to point any moral
 I'll leave that for yourself
 Maybe you're still walking, you're still talking
 You'd like to keep your health
 But every time I read the paper
 Them old feelings come on
 We're waist deep in the Big Muddy
 And the big fool says to push on

We're waist deep in the Big Muddy
And the big fool says to push on *(repeat 1st 2 lines)*
Waist deep! Neck deep!
Soon even a tall man'll be over his head
We're waist deep in the Big Muddy
And the big fool says to push on

Pete Seeger (1967)

This song is a biting piece of political satire where the captain represents President Lyndon B. Johnson, a very large and tall man who continued to insist that the U.S. push forward with its war in Vietnam even in the face of increasing signs of danger. LBJ referred to his doubters about the war as "Nervous Nellies." The 1967 song is prophetic in that continuing over-confident messages from the US military were put to the lie by the Tet Offensive in January 1968.

Pete was invited to appear on *The Smothers Brothers Comedy Hour* in September 1967 - his first appearance on network TV since the blacklist began in 1950. He sang "Waist Deep" during the taping of the show, but CBS decided the song was too hot politically and substituted other material for the song during the actual broadcast. In response to public criticism and pressure from the Smothers Brothers, CBS eventually agreed to let Pete come back on the show a few months later and perform the song as originally planned.

The Water Is Wide

The water is wide, I cannot cross over
And neither have I wings to fly
Give me a boat that can carry two
And both shall row, my love & I

D G D - / Bm Em A - / F♯m - Bm G / D A D -

A ship there is & she sails the sea
She's loaded deep as deep can be
But not so deep as the love I'm in
I know not how I sink or swim

I leaned my back against some young oak
Thinking he was a trusty tree
But first he bended & then he broke
And thus did my false love to me

I put my hand into some soft bush
Thinking the sweetest flower to find
I pricked my finger to the bone
And left the sweetest flower behind

Oh love is handsome & love is fine
Gay as a jewel when first it's new
But love grows old & waxes cold
And fades away like summer dew

The seagulls whirl, they turn & dive
The mountain stands beside the sea
The world we know turns round & round
And all for them & you & me   *(repeat 1st verse)*

Traditional Scottish folk song with additional words & music by Pete Seeger

IF YOU WOULD LIKE TO GET OUT OF A PESSIMISTIC MOOD yourself, I've got a sure remedy for you. Go help those people down in Birmingham, Mississippi or Alabama. All kinds of jobs need to be done. Takes hands & hearts & heads to do it. Human beings to do it. And then we'll see this song come true…

The best verse was made up down in Montgomery, Alabama. Says "We are not afraid." And you & I up here, like every human being in the world, we have been afraid. But you still sing it: "We are not afraid."

- spoken by Pete during his June 8, 1963 Carnegie Hall Concert, recorded live on his "We Shall Overcome" album.

We Shall Overcome

We shall overcome (x2)
We shall overcome some day
Oh deep in my heart I do believe
We shall overcome some day

C F C - (x2) / C FG Am D G D G -
C F C - F G Am - / C F C G C F C -

We'll walk hand in hand...
We shall live in peace...
We shall all be free...
Black & white together...
We are not afraid...today!...
The whole wide world around…

Music & lyrical adaptation by Zilphia Horton, Frank Hamilton, Guy Carawan & Pete Seeger. Inspired by African American gospel singing, members of the Food & Tobacco Workers Union, Charleston SC and the southern Civil Rights Movement.

TRO © 1960 & 1963 (renewed) Ludlow Music Inc. New York NY. All royalties received for this composition are being contributed to the We Shall Overcome Fund & the Freedom Movement under the trusteeship of the writers.

Guy & Candie Carawan, who were directors of the Highlander Center in Tennessee, used the center to offer strong support to the Freedom Movement. Pete spent time with Rev. Martin Luther King Jr. at Highlander in 1957. He & Toshi also took part in the Selma to Montgomery March in 1965. Pete strongly disliked the idea of using his name in copyrighting this song that had sprung so obviously from African American traditions & the Freedom Movement. His manager Harold Leventhal convinced him, however, that copyrighting the song would help protect it from being used commercially or in other ways that might threaten the integrity of the song.

Well May the World Go

Well may the world go
The world go, the world go
Well may the world go
When I'm far away

D - G - / D - A - / 1st / D A D -

Well may the skiers turn
The swimmers churn, the lovers burn
Peace may the generals learn
When I'm far away

Sweet may the fiddle sound
The banjo play the old hoe-down
Dancers swing round & round
When I'm far away

Fresh may the breezes blow
Clear may the streams flow
Blue above, green below
When I'm far away

w: Pete Seeger (1973) m: traditional English ("The Keel Row")

© 1974 (renewed) Stormking Music, Inc. The original song which Seeger used for the tune about a "keel" (boat) is from Northumberland.

The Keel Row

As I went thro' Sandgate, thro' Sandgate, thro' Sandgate
As I went thro' Sandgate, I heard a lassie sing
Weel may the keel row, the keel row, the keel row
Weel may the keel row that ma laddie's in

Traditonal (English folk song)

46

Where Have All the Flowers Gone

Where have all the flowers gone, long time passing?
Where have all the flowers gone, long time ago?
Where have all the flowers gone?
Young girls have picked them every one
When will they ever learn? (2x)

C Am F G (3x) F C / F G C -

Where have all the young girls gone, long time passing?
Where have all the young girls gone, long time ago?
Where have all the young girls gone?
Gone for husbands every one / **When will**…

Where have all the husbands gone…?
Gone for soldiers every one...

Where have all the soldiers gone...?
Gone to graveyards, every one...

Where have all the graveyards gone…?
Gone to flowers, every one...

Pete Seeger (1955) with new verse by Joe Hickerson

PETE WROTE THIS SONG flying on a plane to Oberlin College in 1956. He had in his pocket three lines from the Soviet novel *And Quiet Flows the Don* by Mikhail Sholokhov describing Cossack soldiers riding off to join the Tsar's army:

> "Where are the flowers? The girls have plucked them.
> Where are the girls? They've taken husbands.
> Where are the men? They're all in the army."

These three lines were Pete's original verses. Joe Hickerson (student president of the Oberlin Folksong Club at the time) wrote additional verses which made the story come full circle. Hickerson taught his version to campers at Camp Woodland in 1960 who then sang it around NYC. The Kingston Trio heard the song, thought it was a traditional folk song, and recorded it in 1961. When Pete told them it was his song they gave him credit - along with Joe Hickerson.

Which Side Are You On?

Come all you good workers, good news to you I'll tell
Of how the good old union has come in here to dwell
Which side are you on, boys? which side are you on? (2x)

Am - Em Am / Em Am E Am / Am - E Am /   /

My daddy was a miner & I'm a miner's son
And I'll stick with the union 'til every battle's won

They say in Harlan County, there are no neutrals there
You'll either be a union man or a thug for J. H. Blair

Oh workers, can you stand it? Oh tell me how you can?
Will you be a lousy scab or will you be a man?

Don't scab for the bosses, don't listen to their lies
Us poor folks haven't got a chance unless we organize

Florence Reece (1931)

© 1931 (renewed) Stormking Music, Inc. Reece's tune is an adaptation of the traditional hymn "Lay the Lily Low". This song is one of six union songs The Almanac Singers recorded in 1941, the second of over a hundred recordings Seeger eventually made. The Almanac Singers included Lee Hays (later one Pete's fellow Weavers), Millard Lampell, and Woody Guthrie.

"WHICH SIDE ARE YOU ON?" is a miners' song written in 1932 in the midst of the bitter struggles of the miners in Harlan County, Kentucky. The mine owners, unyielding in their opposition to any unionization of the workers, carried on a campaign of violence and terror to smash the union. At least a dozen miners were killed by deputies hired by the operators, but none of the deputies were indicted.

The song was written during one of the many terroristic raids by the sheriff [J.H.Blair] and his deputies on the miners' homes. They came to the home of Sam Reece, one of the leaders of the National Miners' Union, but he had been warned in time and escaped. They poked their shotguns everywhere, under the beds and into the closets, even into the piles of dirty linen, searching for the miners' leader. When Reece's young daughters, aged 8 and 11, started crying, one of the deputies laughed and said: "What are you crying for? We don't want you. We're after your old man."

After the deputies had left, Mrs. Florence Reece, wife of the rank & file leader, was seething with indignation. She tore an old calendar off the wall and on the back side wrote the verses of the great labor song, which she put to the tune of an old Baptist hymn she had known from childhood. The song was immediately picked up by the striking miners after it had been sung at the union hall by Mrs. Reece's two little girls. From Harlan County it spread throughout the entire labor movement.

A few of the verses of the song were slightly changed later by the Almanac Singers: [The 2nd verse above] originally read:

> "My daddy was a miner, he's now in the air & sun
> He'll be with you fellow workers until this battle's won."

The words "He's now in the air & sun" refer to the fact that he was blacklisted from work. - *Philip S. Foner (from the liner notes to the Folkways LP "Talking Union & Other Union Songs").*

IN THE NEXT FEW PAGES we have included five of the many terrific songs that have been written to celebrate Pete's vision, music, and struggles for peace, justice, and the earth. Visit www.groupsinging.org/seeger/songs-about to see a list of some of the other great songs about Pete, including "It's Pete" by his sister Peggy.

High Over the Hudson

The news came over the air tonight
Pete Seeger went sailing today
Set out on the Hudson 'bout 9 o'clock
Searching for new songs to play
   Passed by Bear Mountain, making great time
   As the water slapped hard on the bow
   At Storm King he turned that boat into the wind
   Set the old "Woody G" on the prow! Now he's:

(in 3/4) G - / Em - / Am - / F D :∥

High over the Hudson
Sails headed for home
Hard on the breeze as it cuts thru the trees
Pete, you're not sailing alone
   You're high over the Hudson
   You've got one hell of a view
   Your battles are won, a new journey's begun
   Pete, we're singing with you (*last time add:* with you)

G - / Em - / Am F / Am D :∥ (last time add G -)

The troubadour's life has its ups & its downs
Of that, there's so much that's been said
Pete spoke out for justice, year after year
A leader who actually led
   He sang out for freedom, he sang out for peace
   Taught thru the power of song
   Ahead of his time in all seasons of life
   He kept us all singing along! And he's:

Odetta & Mary say "Welcome good friend!"
And Woody & Faith both agree
That you lived your passion for 94 years
And you lived it with integrity

Now we as your children and we as your friends
Take up your mission of song
As Toshi yells out, with a smile on her lips
"Hey, Peter, what took you so long!" / And you're...

Reggie Harris

Let Me Sing You a Song

You've asked me here to tell you about my neighbors & my friends
To talk about the who & what, the where & how & when
But I won't give you anything you don't already know
But if you'd like I'll sing that list of songs before I go

C - F - / G - F C :∥

Let me sing you a song about the people that I love
The poets & philosophers, the workers & the wanderers
The ones who walk the picket lines who dare to stand & fight
And the ones who hold their babies close & rock them
    through the night

C - F - / G - F C / C - F - / G - FG C -

Well you say it's un-American to do the things I do
Well I sing for justice, liberty & Civil Rights it's true
But I say it's un-American to ask me how I vote
How I pray or what I believe but here's a song I wrote

If you want to send me to prison, I guess that's the way it'll be
'Cause I won't give you fodder for your paranoid machine
If the price of my silence is shackles, well then fellas, take me away
For I will live to sing again & rise with a brand new day

Joe Jencks

Sing People Sing

When I was four I had a toy made of plastic & of joy
A magic, musical machine from a drum, a stick & strings
I couldn't know as I would play, I'd live to meet the man one day
Playing songs that shaped my life & taught the world to sing

(up 4) G ↓ C G / C G C D / 1st / C G CD G

Oh hear the banjo ring / Hear the people sing
Hope changes everything / Sing, people, sing!

D - C G / C D G - / D C G Em / C D G -

The summer of my 18th year in San Francisco he'd appear
I jumped onto a trolley car alone & wondering
The "grove" was full when I got there,
    people came from everywhere
I climbed a redwood by the stage to watch the revelling

Years went by I got a call, a festival in early Fall
Along the Hudson River shore, a harvest gathering
Asking me to volunteer to keep the river clean & clear
To celebrate the river's life & all the gifts she brings

(bridge) You stood up to McCarthy's rage, rallied for a living wage
Rode with Woody, marched with Dr. King
You patiently brought us along, taught us each & every song
With Toshi by your side you could do most anything

Em - A - / C D G - / 1st / C - D -

You showed us how the world could be, living with integrity
Together we create a force beyond imagining
As I observed your dimming light I felt a spark in me ignite
But I would trade it all today to hear your banjo ring

Pat Humphries & Sandy O

Spoon of Sand

Spoon of sand can tip the balance
Drops of water turn a mill
Way out here over the rainbow
Someone's standing, singing still

(up 2) C - F - / G - C - / 1st / C G C -

You weathered the storm, you finished the race
We see by the weary smile upon your face
You've stumbled & risen, you sang up the dawn
You kindled the fire, you carried the torch, you're passing it on

G - C - / / F - Em - / C G C -

Dark clouds on the mountain, dead fish on the shore
The bottom-line bankers, the vultures of war
You turn & you face them & when push comes to shove
Somehow you believe hate has to surrender, surrounded by love

You charted the waters, saw the river run clear
You raised the sail when we thought the journey
    would end in despair
At the darkest hour on the edge of the dawn
You caught the 1st light & gave us the vision to carry it on

Charlie King

© 2014 Charlie King, Pied Asp Music (BMI). Pete envisioned the great problems of the world as a bucket of rocks riveted on one end of a seesaw. On the other end, an empty bucket. But if enough people, one by one, put enough spoons of sand in the empty bucket, one day - zoop! - the balance shifts, the problem is overcome. This song celebrates that vision and the life Pete lived.

We'll Pass Them On

When you're gone **(who will sing?)** (x2)
When you're gone who will sing your songs?
You have planted the simple seed of singing in our hearts
And we'll sing them with each other as we pass them on

D - G -/ D - A -/ D D⁷ G -/ D - A D

    We'll pass **(pass them on)** them on **(pass them on)**
    We'll sing **(pass them on)** your songs **(pass...)**
    You have planted the simple seed of singing in our hearts
    And we'll sing them with each other as we pass them on

A - D -/   / D D⁷ G -/ D - A D

When <u>we're</u> gone **(who will sing?)** (2x)
When we're gone who will sing <u>our</u> songs?
We will plant the simple seed of singing <u>in the world</u>
And we'll sing them with the children who will pass them on
    <u>They'll</u> pass **(pass them on)** them on **(pass...)**
    They'll sing **(pass...)** <u>our</u> songs **(pass...)**
    We will plant the simple seed of singing in the world
    And we'll sing them with the children who will pass them on

When <u>they're</u> gone **(who will sing?)** (2x)
When they're gone who will sing <u>their</u> songs?
They will plant the simple seed of singing <u>on the wind</u>
And the children of the future, they will pass them on
    They'll pass **(pass them on)** them on **(pass...)**
    They'll sing **(pass...)** <u>their</u> songs **(pass...)**
    They will plant the simple seed of singing on the wind
    And the children of the future, they will pass them on

Sally Rogers

～ Postscript ～
Love Call Me Home

When the waters are deep
Friends carry me over
When I cry in my sleep
Love call me home

(up 3) C Am / F G :∥

Time, ferry me down the river
Friends carry me safely over
Life, tend me on my journey
Love call me home

C - / F G :∥

When the waters are cold
Friends carry me over
When I'm losing my hold
Love call me home

When I'm weary & cannot swim
Friends carry me over
Open your arms & take me in
Love call me home

Take the gift I bring
Friends carry me over
Deep within me life is singing
Love call me home

Life offers a chance for friends to carry us over
Time can stop or dance forever
Love call me home

Peggy Seeger

SUBJECT INDEX